Thomas Nast

Honesty in the Pursuit
of Corruption

Other Titles in the Series

Rachel Carson: Perseverance to Save the Planet
By Ann Waldron
Marie Curie: Honesty in Science
By Carl Rollyson
Charles Darwin: Working for the Love of Science
By Steve Kemper
Emily Dickinson: Self-Discipline in the Service of Art
By Lisa Paddock
Galileo: Perseverance in the Cause of Truth
By Michael Golay
Thor Heyerdahl: Courage Under Fire
By Colin Evans
The Mercury Astronauts: Courage at the Cutting Edge
By Marshall Riggan

Sofwest Press
Las Cruces, NM, USA

LIVES WORTH LIVING

Thomas Nast

Honesty in the Pursuit of Corruption

by

Richard Worth

The Lives Worth Living *Series consists of biographies of men and women whose lives illustrate one or more primary virtues or aspects of good character. The books are written for the young reader in middle school or junior high and include critical thinking questions, a summary chapter, and afterword to parents. The facts and events recorded in this book are true and based upon the most reliable research sources available. However, the author has dramatized some scenes and dialogue to make the text more readable. In such cases, every effort was made to build the dialogue on a foundation of the known facts and the character of the subject.*

Produced by New England Publishing Associates, Inc. for SOFSOURCE, Inc.

Series Editor: Edward W. Knappman
Copy Editing: Miccinello Associates
Design and Page Composition: Ron Formica
Photo Researcher: Victoria Harlow
Editorial Administration: Ron Formica and Chris Ceplenski
Proofreading: Doris Troy

Cover Design: Gabriel Quesada
Cover Photo: Organ Mountains at Sunrise, Las Cruces, NM; Frank Parrish

ISBN 1-57163-604-8

Library of Congress Catalog Card Number: 98-84203
Printed in the United States of America
01 00 99 98   9 8 7 6 5 4 3 2 1

Table of Contents

TIMELINE viii

Prologue 1
HONESTY

Chapter 1 5
COMING TO AMERICA

Chapter 2 13
THE CIVIL WAR

Chapter 3 23
POKING FUN AT THE POWERFUL

Chapter 4 33
TWEED AND TAMMANY

Chapter 5 44
THE FALL OF BOSS TWEED

Chapter 6 51
AN ARTIST'S WORLD

Chapter 7 59
A FORGOTTEN MAN

Epilogue 63
SUMMING UP A LIFE

AFTERWORD TO PARENTS 65

BIBLIOGRAPHY 67

GLOSSARY 69

Timeline

Biographical Milestone	Year	Historical Milestone
1840: Thomas Nast is born in Landau, Germany.	**1840**	**1840s:** Famines grip Europe, causing thousands to emigrate to America.
1846: The Nast family arrives in New York City and finds a home there.		
		1848: California gold rush begins.
	1850	
1854: Nast's father dies.		**1854:** The Republican Party is formed as an antislavery party in Jackson, Michigan.
1856: Thomas Nast goes to work for *Leslie's Illustrated Weekly Newspaper.*		
1859: Nast goes to work for the *New York Illustrated News.*		**Oct. 16, 1859:** John Brown conducts his raid on Harper's Ferry, Virginia.
1860: Nast draws pictures of Giuseppe Garibaldi's victories in Italy.	**1860**	
1861: Sarah Edwards and Thomas Nast marry.		**1861:** The Civil War begins.
1862: Nast joins *Harper's Weekly* and draws pictures of the Civil War. He also introduces the modern portrayal of Santa Claus.		
		April 14, 1865: President Abraham Lincoln is assassinated.
1868: Nast supports Ulysses S. Grant's election as president of the United States.		
1869: Nast begins drawing his caricatures of New York City political boss William M. Tweed.		

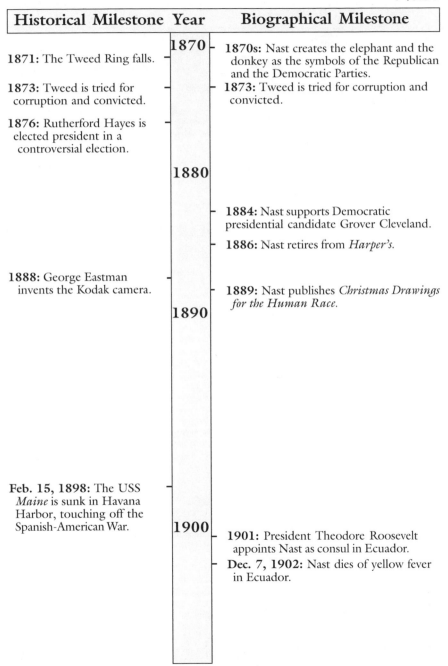

Historical Milestone	Year	Biographical Milestone
1871: The Tweed Ring falls.	**1870**	**1870s:** Nast creates the elephant and the donkey as the symbols of the Republican and the Democratic Parties.
1873: Tweed is tried for corruption and convicted.		**1873:** Tweed is tried for corruption and convicted.
1876: Rutherford Hayes is elected president in a controversial election.		
	1880	
		1884: Nast supports Democratic presidential candidate Grover Cleveland.
		1886: Nast retires from *Harper's*.
1888: George Eastman invents the Kodak camera.		**1889:** Nast publishes *Christmas Drawings for the Human Race*.
	1890	
Feb. 15, 1898: The USS *Maine* is sunk in Havana Harbor, touching off the Spanish-American War.	**1900**	**1901:** President Theodore Roosevelt appoints Nast as consul in Ecuador.
		Dec. 7, 1902: Nast dies of yellow fever in Ecuador.

Prologue

HONESTY

*T*here is an old proverb that states: "The pen is mightier than the sword." Thomas Nast (1840–1902) proved that this proverb is true.

With his pen and pencil, Nast became the most famous cartoonist in the nineteenth century. The powerful pictures he drew between 1861 and 1865 helped the Union win the Civil War. Nast's drawings persuaded many men to join the Army. He also convinced the people at home to support their troops in blue.

During the 1870s, Nast's cartoons brought down the most powerful group of corrupt politicians in

America. This was the Tweed Ring, named after William Marcy Tweed, the political boss of New York. They thought no one could stop them. But Nast did.

Nast's guiding principle was honesty. Others might be afraid in the face of corruption and do nothing. But Nast was too honest to be stopped. He drew things as he saw them. Sometimes his honesty proved very dangerous. His life was threatened by the politicians he was trying to expose. But Nast continued to draw his cartoons.

Nast's success illustrates the power of the press in the nineteenth century. As literacy spread, more and more people began to read newspapers, especially in large cities like New York. Through his drawings, he influenced his readers and showed them how corrupt their politicians were. Once people learned the truth from Nast's drawings, they went to the polls and voted the corrupt politicians out of office.

Of course, Thomas Nast wasn't perfect. He could sometimes be extremely intolerant of people who disagreed with him. And he would lampoon them mercilessly in his cartoons.

To Nast all things were either black or white. There was nothing in between.

—Thomas Nast St. Hill (grandson), 1971

But friends often overlooked this flaw and remembered Nast for his unflinching honesty, the quality that enabled him to have a tremendous impact on his times. Today, we recall Thomas Nast as a symbol of fearless journalism — a man who was unafraid to stand up for his beliefs.

Points to Ponder

◆ Do you see a connection between honesty and courage? How did Nast exemplify courage?

◆ Do you think journalists today are generally honest and fair?

◆ Do you know someone personally who has shown both honesty and courage in his or her own way?

Chapter 1

❊

COMING TO
AMERICA

long the narrow, dusty roads of Germany, horse carts headed toward the points where ships left cross the Atlantic. Each cart carried a family, along with boxes of their clothes and other valuables, on a journey that would eventually take them to a new land. In 1846, there was famine in Germany. The potato crop had failed, leaving thousands of people dying of starvation and threatening the lives of many more. Farmers decided they had endured enough, so they packed up their families as well as their belongings and departed. Teachers, craftsmen and artisans left too, believing they could earn far more in America than the meager salaries they were being paid at home.

Among the people who emigrated to America were the Nasts. They came from Landau, a small German town with an army base. The family consisted of Joseph Nast, a poorly paid trombonist in the army, his wife, Apollonia, and their children. Among them was a six-year-old boy named Thomas. Although Joseph had not yet finished his army enlistment, he decided that his family should go to America ahead of him. Once they were established there, he would join them after his German army service was over.

For Thomas the trip was both sad and exciting. He was excited about going to a new country, but he regretted leaving his friends and father behind. As Apollonia and her children continued their journey, they passed through Strasbourg, a bustling city in eastern France. Finally, they arrived in the French seaport of Le Havre on the Atlantic Ocean. There, emigrants often had to wait several weeks or months for a ship to arrive that would take them to America. Meanwhile, they lived in ramshackle apartment buildings with hundreds of other families. Bands of thieves lurked in the streets of Le Havre, so emigrants had to protect their possessions carefully or they would be stolen.

From Le Havre, the voyage aboard a sailing ship to America lasted about fifty to sixty days. If the crossing was rough, passengers often suffered from violent seasickness. Emigrant families were often crowded together, receiving only meager amounts of food and living in unsanitary conditions. As a result, outbreaks of smallpox and cholera sometimes occured aboard ship that took the lives of some emigrants before they ever reached the United States.

Fortunately, the Nasts arrived safely at their destination — New York. As their ship arrived in the harbor, it would have pulled alongside scores of other vessels — tall-masted schooners, steamboats with their huge paddle wheels, ferryboats and cargo ships. New York was the busiest harbor in America, as well as its largest city, with a population of approximately 350,000. Some New Yorkers worked in the city's banks and brokerage firms on Wall Street; others were employed in huge department stores on Broadway, like Lord and Taylor; and still others ran butcher shops, bakeries and restaurants.

Many of the people who lived in New York were recent immigrants, like the Nasts. By the 1840s, there were already large groups of Italians, Irish and Germans living there. Indeed, by this time almost 100,000 Germans lived in the city.

Thomas Nast first visited Castle Garden during the 1850s to sketch various performers, including singer Jenny Lind.

The Nasts found a home on the east side of the city in lower Manhattan. And Thomas began attending school. Since he spoke hardly a word of English, Thomas had a difficult time understanding the subjects being taught. But even when his English improved, Thomas admitted that he was still a very poor student. Instead, he preferred to spend his time doing something that seemed far more satisfying — drawing pictures.

For someone who possessed a natural artistic gift, New York provided hundreds of interesting subjects, and Tom began sketching them. In one of his earliest pictures, Tom drew Coney Island. This was a popular amusement park with a beach, a long boardwalk and many restaurants, which attracted thousands of people during the summer.

Tom's father finally came to America in 1850 and played part time in a band at a local theater. Tom would sometimes attend performances and sketch the actors as they played their roles. He also went to Castle Garden, a huge auditorium in lower New York, to see the famous singer Jenny Lind. Indeed, he even sketched Miss Lind as she stood onstage and sang to the standing-room-only crowd.

The low and middle notes of her voice are superb, and the high notes as good as such notes can be. . . . None of her portraits do her justice . . . there's an air about her of dignity, self-possession, modesty, and goodness that is extremely attractive.

—George Templeton Strong, diarist, commenting on
Jenny Lind's performance, 1850

Tom's parents recognized his artistic talent, and eventually enrolled him in a drawing class so he could improve his skills. In the same building were the studios of several New York artists. One of them, Alfred Fredericks, took an interest in Tom and arranged for him to be admitted to the Academy of Design. This was a well-known art school where Tom could receive the training he needed to become a professional artist.

Unfortunately, his training at the academy did not last very long. In 1854, his father died and fourteen-year-old Tom needed to find a job to help support the Nast family. By this time he had put together a portfolio of his sketches and decided to apply for a position as an artist at one of the city's newspapers. Eventually, he approached Frank Leslie, the formidable owner of *Leslie's Illustrated Weekly Newspaper.*

"What makes you think you're an artist?" Leslie asked, glaring down at Tom. The newspaper editor was a very tall man who wore glasses that sat on the end of his nose.

"As you can see," Tom replied, showing Leslie his portfolio, "I do know how to draw."

"Humph," Leslie said turning over the pictures. "That doesn't mean you can work for my newspaper."

"All I ask is a chance," Tom stammered.

"Okay," Leslie said with a chuckle. "Let's see what you can do. Go down to the harbor when all the people are rushing to find a seat on the ferryboat after work and draw what you see. Then I'll decide whether it's good enough to print in my newspaper."

Tom left the editor's office and marched down the street to the harbor. There were so many people that at first Tom wasn't too sure he could decide which ones to include in his picture. But at last his eye fixed on some of them — men in their high hats, a few women in their heavy coats and even a boy with his dog. Much to Leslie's surprise, Tom passed the test. His sketch was then reproduced in the newspaper. And Tom was hired for $4 a week.

At this time, photography was still in its infancy, so Americans relied on artists' sketches to illustrate the important events of the day on the pages of their newspapers. Some of Nast's early pictures for *Leslie's* exposed corruption scandals in the city. One of them involved milk dealers who were selling milk from diseased cows. Another exposed graft on the police force, showing officers extorting money from patrolmen. In these sketches Nast began to demonstrate the fearless honesty

. . . gaunt and shivering forms and wild ghastly faces [in] hideous squalor . . . a tin pail of lighted charcoal placed in the center of the room, over which bent a blind man endeavoring to warm himself . . . in one corner of the floor, a woman who had died the day previous of disease.

—contemporary newspaper account of slum conditions in the 1850s that would mark so many of his pictures. Working for a newspaper, he believed, involved a responsibility to tell the truth. He tried to make that truth vivid and bring it alive, so his readers would understand it.

In 1859, Nast left *Leslie's* and went to work for the *New York Illustrated News,* which offered him a better salary. Working at this newspaper, he exposed the terrible conditions in the city's tenement buildings. In some areas of the city, such as Five Points, poor immigrant families were crowded into a single room, often with no heat, very little food and only a few pieces of furniture. Nast graphically showed these terrible slums in his pictures.

Thomas Nast's career as a crusading artist had begun.

Points to Ponder

◆ Can you think of examples of political corruption today?

◆ Whom do you think political corruption hurts the most?

◆ Do you think words or pictures are more powerful in exposing wrongdoing?

Chapter 2

❧

THE CIVIL WAR

In 1860, Thomas Nast was in England, where he had been sent by his newspaper to draw pictures of a famous boxing match. The bout involved John Heenan, an American champion, and Tom Sayers, England's best fighter. Nast had covered one of Heenan's earlier fights, and the two had become good friends. In April, he sketched the English match, which went forty-two rounds. Each of the men fought with bare knuckles, until

THE CHAMPIONSHIP FIGHT BETWEEN HEENAN AND SAYERS, ON APRIL 17, 1860
Jack Macdonald   Billy Mulligan   Joseph Cusick   The " Benicia Boy "   Thomas Sayers   Morrissey   Jemmy Welsh Harry Brunton
From a sketch by our artist, Thomas Nast, Esq.   Engraved by A. V. S. Anthony, Esq., on board the " Vanderbilt," on her return passage.
(Reproduced from double-page cut in the New York Illustrated News)

On April 17, 1860, Thomas Nast sketched the boxing match between England's noted fighter Tom Sayers and America's John Heenan, a contest that lasted forty-two rounds.

one of them could no longer continue fighting. Heenan finally won.

After completing this assignment, Nast wanted to travel to Italy to cover the military campaigns of Giuseppe Garibaldi — an Italian patriot who wanted to unite his country and free it from rule by foreign powers. This was just the type of man who appealed to Nast's crusading spirit. But Nast didn't have any money. His newspaper was late in paying him.

"I'll loan you twenty pounds from my prize money," Heenan told him.

"But I don't know when I can pay you back," Nast said.

"That's all right," Heenan assured him, and handed him the cash.

The young artist joined Garibaldi's march through southern Italy. Nast sketched several fierce battles involving Garibaldi's army, called the Red Shirts, as well as his liberation of Naples. So enthusiastic was Nast that he even wore a hat and a red shirt just like Garibaldi's.

While he was in Europe, Nast had been corresponding with a woman named Sarah Edwards. Before leaving for England, Thomas had picnicked with Sarah along the Hudson River and painted scenery for an amateur play staged at Sarah's house. In 1861, after returning to America, Thomas married Sarah and they spent their honeymoon at Niagara Falls. This was a popular spot for newly married couples who would walk along the Niagara River and gaze at the falls crashing thunderously nearby.

The year 1861 also marked the beginning of the Civil War. Staunchly pro-Union and anti-slavery, Tom was soon covering the momentous events of the day for his newspaper. He drew president-elect Abraham Lincoln's arrival in New York City and followed him to Washington, D.C.

In 1862, Nast moved to another newspaper, *Harper's Weekly,* which sent him out to cover the battles between Union and Confederate troops. Nast's experience in Italy gave him a general knowledge of battlefield tactics as well as an understanding of how to draw military engagements.

At the battle of Antietam, in 1862, bullets were flying through the air and cannon were roaring across the battlefield. Long lines of Union soldiers marched forward and fought the Confederate enemy in fierce hand-to-hand combat. Tom tried to hold his pencil firmly, but he was scared. One of those bullets might hit him before he could ever finish his picture. Nearby, men were cut in two from cannon blasts. Others fell from sniper fire. A cavalry troop galloped past Tom on its way to the front. But he kept sketching. A few days later his picture appeared on the cover of *Harper's.*

Thomas Nast has been our best recruiting sergeant.

—Abraham Lincoln

Thomas Nast … did as much as any one man to preserve the Union and bring the war to an end.

—Ulysses S. Grant

But the artist's most famous work was more than just pictures of battles. Nast tried to tell a story with a moral message. He was devoted to the Northern cause,

Thomas Nast drew "The War in the Border States," which appeared in Harper's Weekly *on January 17, 1863. He portrayed the destruction of the Civil War in the South and the kindness of Union soldiers who helped the victims.*

but in the early part of the war many Northerners had grave doubts about Lincoln's ability to lead the country to victory. Nast's drawings were designed to increase support for the Union war effort and to encourage men to join the Army and fight against the South.

One of his pictures, "The War in the Border States," shows the horror of warfare for the people whose homes were destroyed in the conflict. It also portrays the warm, generous spirit of the Union soldiers who helped them. Another picture — "The Emancipation of the Negroes, January, 1863" — shows Nast's enthusiastic support for Lincoln's decision to free the slaves.

Nast also demonstrated his understanding of the Union fighting men and their families. In one picture, published over the Christmas holiday in 1862, he shows several children nestled in their bed, while their mother sits by the window waiting for her husband — a Union soldier who is away at war.

As the Civil War continued, Thomas Nast used his artist's pen to influence the people of the North. Nast was a man with very strong opinions. Part of his reputation for honesty was based on his willingness to state those opinions — even if others might disagree with him. In short, he had the courage of his convictions, and he expressed them through his pictures and caricatures.

A caricature is a picture that exaggerates the people or events it portrays. An artist uses caricatures to express his point of view. Europe had produced a number of great caricaturists, such as Honoré Daumier in France. But Thomas Nast was the first great American caricaturist. Indeed, some experts think that no one has ever surpassed his work. Nast used his caricatures very skillfully to sway the attitudes and beliefs of the people who read *Harper's*.

In 1864, Abraham Lincoln ran for reelection against Democrat George B. McClellan. Nast was convinced McClellan's election would be the worst thing that could happen to the Union. He believed that the Democrats would end the war and let the Confederacy remain an independent nation. During the election, Nast created a famous picture for *Harper's* called "Compromise with

Nast Enlists Santa in the Union Cause

Nast is perhaps best known for a series of drawings that first appeared in the 1862 Christmas issue of *Harper's*. It shows Santa Claus bringing presents to the Union troops. This was the first time the portrayal of Santa, as we know him today, appeared in America. His picture was actually inspired by a poem written forty years earlier by Professor Clement Moore. Titled "A Visit from Saint Nicholas," Moore's famous poem begins this way:

> 'Twas the night before Christmas
> When all through the house
> Not a creature was stirring,
> Not even a mouse.

Nast portrays Santa Claus the way Moore described him:

> His eyes how they twinkled! His dimples
> how merry!
> His cheeks were like roses, his nose like a
> cherry ...
> He had a broad face and a little round
> belly
> That shook, when he laughed, like a
> bowl full of jelly.

One of Thomas Nast's most noted drawings is "Compromise with the South," which he created for Harper's Weekly. *It was published on September 3, 1864.*

the South." The Republicans used this picture during the presidential campaign, and it helped reelect Lincoln.

In 1865, the South surrendered. But only five days later, Lincoln was assassinated at Ford's Theater in Washington by John Wilkes Booth. Nast summed up the feelings of a nation when he showed a tearful Columbia — a tall, robed woman who symbolized the United States — with her head bowed beside Lincoln's coffin. With Lincoln's death, one phase of Nast's career had come to an end. He was now America's best-known popular artist and only twenty-five years old. But an even more important part of his life was just beginning.

Points to Ponder

◆ Would you describe Nast's Civil War illustrations as journalism or war propaganda?

◆ What examples of successful caricatures have you seen recently in newspapers or magazines?

Chapter 3

POKING FUN
AT THE POWERFUL

fter the Civil War, Thomas Nast turned his artist's pencil to new subjects. For the first time he began to draw caricatures of the rich, the famous and the powerful. In fact, one of the prime targets of his satire was the president of the United States — Andrew Johnson.

Born in North Carolina, Johnson had received almost no formal schooling when he moved to Greeneville Tennessee, to open a tailor's shop. Eventually, he entered politics, becoming mayor of Greeneville, and later congressman and senator from his home state. When the Civil War broke out, the people of Tennessee werg almost evenly divided between those favoring the Union and those supporting the new Confederacy. Johnson stood by the Union. Abraham Lincoln appointed Johnson military governor of Tennessee, and he helped defend the state capital, Nashville, during a Confederate siege. In 1864, he was chosen to be Lincoln's vice president, assuming the presidency when Lincoln was assassinated.

After the war's end, Johnson wanted to bring the Southern states back into the Union with as little bitterness as possible. This was part of a process known as Reconstruction. He issued pardons to all the Confederate leaders and called on Southerners to immediately elect new congressmen and senators to come to Washington. But in the meantime, the Southern politicians were restricting the rights of the newly freed African-American slaves. They prevented them from voting and passed laws that made it difficult for them to climb out of poverty.

The Republicans, who controlled Congress, were outraged at what Johnson was allowing the South to do. And Thomas Nast agreed with them. In 1866, forty-eight African Americans were killed by white police during a riot in New Orleans.

Nast took up his pen and portrayed the event for the readers of *Harper's*. He showed Johnson as a Roman emperor and compared the African Americans to the Christians in ancient Rome who were killed for entertainment in the Coliseum. In another cartoon, Nast portrayed Johnson as "King Andrew" vetoing the legislation that the Republican Congress tried to impose on the South.

Nast had seen the horrors of the Civil War, and he wanted to ensure that the conflict had not been fought for nothing. This meant extending equality to African Americans throughout the South. In 1866, Congress passed the Fourteenth Amendment, which guarantees these rights. But it was not popular. Some Southerners, for example, formed the Ku Klux Klan and selected Confederate general Nathan Bedford Forrest as the first leader, or Grand Wizard. Riding horses across the landscape at night in their white sheets and white hoods, Klan members terrorized African Americans. During one three-month period, for instance, sixty-three African Americans were killed in Mississippi.

Nast deplored these actions. In one cartoon, drawn just after the end of the Civil War, he shows African Americans being denied the vote. Another picture shows an African-American family cowering below a hooded member of the Klan. Nast was very outspoken in his beliefs, which were not universally accepted by the readers of *Harper's*. Although African Americans had lived in freedom throughout the North long before the Civil War, many Northerners looked on them as second-class citizens. To Nast, whites and African Americans were equal. And his conscience required him to honestly express this belief in his pictures.

NOBODY'S PERFECT

Nast's support of voting rights for African Americans was also motivated by politics. He firmly believed that if their right to vote was protected, African Americans would be grateful to the Republican Party. And they would vote for Republicans. Nast was an ardent Republican. He believed the party was responsible for abolishing slavery and winning the Civil War. And he wanted to see it remain in control of Congress as well as the White House. A majority of Southern whites, on the other hand, supported the Democratic Party. By giving the vote to African Americans, Republicans thought they could keep the Democrats out of power.

In 1868, Republicans were planning to meet in Chicago to nominate a president. Andrew Johnson no longer had the support of his party. Instead, they were thinking of someone who was far more popular with voters — the hero of the Civil War, Ulysses S. Grant.

This drawing portrays Andrew Johnson as a Roman emperor. Entitled "Amphitheatrum Johnsonianum — Massacre of the Innocents at New Orleans," it was published in Harper's Weekly *on July 30, 1866.*

"Grant should be the nominee," Nast said to his wife Sarah, as they sat together over breakfast one morning. "He's done so much for this country. How can I make sure the convention supports him?"

Sarah often helped Tom with his caricatures and even thought up captions for some of them. "You'll just have to show everyone that he's the best man for the job," she told her husband.

"But how can I do that with a single picture?"

"Why don't you put Grant on a pedestal and next to it draw another one that's empty? Then

Columbia could be pointing to Grant and underneath would be the caption: 'Match him!' " Sarah said.

Nast loved the idea. "That will show everyone that no one can match Grant."

Nast traveled to Chicago and painted the picture on a curtain at the back of the convention hall. The picture was hidden behind a blank curtain. Then the curtain was raised and the picture shown to a convention hall of wildly cheering delegates who were supporting Grant for president. Later it was published by *Harper's*.

Perhaps it seems unusual for a newspaperman like Nast to play such a partisan role in the convention of a political party. Today, journalists are expected to be fair and to report the news without showing support for either party. But the nineteenth century was different. Newspapers were regularly identified as strongly Democratic or Republican. And their cartoonists were expected to express strong opinions about political candidates.

Two things elected me, the sword of Sheridan and the pencil of Thomas Nast.

—Ulysses S. Grant, 1868

When Thomas Nast drew a picture of Governor Seymour speaking during the election campaign in New York, he placed two small horns atop his head, making him look like a devil.

The Democrats did try to match Grant by nominating Horatio Seymour, the governor of New York, as their candidate. During the election campaign, Nast drew Seymour with little horns that made him look like the devil. By contrast, he portrayed Grant as a great war hero. During the election, Grant traveled to several states accompanied by generals, such as Philip H. Sheridan, who had helped him win the Civil War. There were huge torchlight parades with great crowds of Union veterans marching in support of the man who had brought them victory. The result was a landslide that swept Ulysses S. Grant into the White House.

Grant served as president for eight years. Ironically, his administration is remembered chiefly for its level of corruption. There is no evidence that Grant himself ever had a hand in any of the dishonest dealings that occurred during his presidency. But he did little to stop them. Many of the politicians were his friends, and Grant believed in remaining loyal to them.

Nast remained loyal to Grant. No matter what happened around the embattled president, Nast usually portrayed him as personally honest and upright — a victim of circumstances. And he often attacked those who would bring his hero down. In 1872, for example, the Republicans wanted to nominate someone to replace Grant as president. Leading the Republican rebels was Senator Carl Schurz of Missouri.

Like Nast, Schurz was German-born. Schurz was a tall man with very long legs, and Nast enjoyed drawing caricatures of him in *Harper's*. In one cartoon, he is shown as a member of a pirate crew, which is leading the ship of state in the wrong direction. Schurz warned Nast to stop his attacks. And *Harper's* editor, George William Curtis, tried to put pressure on him to change his position.

"I am confounded and chagrined by your picture of this week," Curtis wrote him, "in which my personal friends and those whom I asked you to spare are exposed to what I think is not only ridicule but injustice."

But Nast was adamant. Grant was not only renominated but also reelected in 1872. And part of the credit was due to Thomas Nast, who ridiculed his Democratic opponent, Horace Greeley.

Nast, you more than any other man have won a . . . victory for Grant — I mean, for Civilization and Progress.

—Mark Twain, 1872

Unfortunately, the scandals in Grant's second administration only grew worse. Grant's secretary, Orville Babcock, took payoffs from a ring of liquor distillers who bribed public officials to avoid taxes. And Grant's secretary of war resigned when he was caught taking a bribe from a dishonest merchant who was seeking control over an Indian trading post.

Nevertheless, Nast stood by his hero. In 1876, one of his cartoons showed Grant as a lion sitting in the president's chair, being unfairly treated as a scapegoat that is having to bear the burden of responsibility for any and all corruption in his administration. Although the country might blame Grant for everything, Nast continued to believe that Grant was personally honest, just as Nast himself was. Indeed, the artist and the president always remained close friends.

Points to Ponder

◆ Do you think journalists should take sides in politics the way Nast did?

◆ Sometimes we overlook faults in our friends that we clearly see in others, just as Nast did with President Grant. Can you think of examples when you may have done the same thing?

Chapter 4

TWEED AND
TAMMANY

*T*homas Nast's world was inhabited by the heroes and villains he drew in his cartoons. If President Grant was one of Nast's heroes, then his arch villain was William Marcy Tweed.

A three-hundred-pound, six-foot-tall giant of a man, Tweed had grown up in the rough and tumble of the

This Nathaniel Currier lithograph depicts the terrific explosion at the great fire in New York on July 19, 1845. (Courtesy: CIGNA Museum and Art Collection, Philadelphia, Pa.)

New York City streets and eventually became the boss of Democratic politics. Tweed got his start as a fire fighter.

During the nineteenth century, fires were common in New York, where so many buildings were made of wood. In 1845, the year before Nast came to America, a fire had destroyed three hundred buildings and caused $6 million worth of damage. The blaze raged for a week before it was finally over.

To deal with these fires, the city relied on volunteer fire companies. There was heated competition among the companies to determine who would have the honor of putting out a blaze. As each company pulled its pump engine to the site of a fire, fights would break out as firemen from one engine company tried to prevent men of another company from getting to the burning building ahead of them. Sometimes the building would burn down while the firemen were still fighting with each other. One of the best-known companies was the Americus Fire Engine Company Number Six, led by William Marcy Tweed.

Tweed was a bookkeeper in a brush-making company. But this job was much too dull to satisfy him. He was a big, burly brawler who loved fighting other engine companies as much as he did fires. He was also a natural leader who took his famous engine company on a national tour in 1851. The firemen wore red shirts, shiny black hats and fancy suspenders. Their engine was emblazoned with the symbol of a fierce tiger. Their trip included stops in Baltimore and Philadelphia as well as a visit to the White House, where they were presented to President Millard Fillmore.

While he was a volunteer fireman, Tweed had also joined Tammany Hall. This was the headquarters of the Tammany Society, the center of Democratic politics in New York City. Tammany was the name of an Indian chief, and the hall where its members met was a long room in a hotel built in 1812. It was known as the Wigwam. Over the years, Tammany had become extremely effective at organizing voters — which became a major source of its immense power.

When immigrants arrived in New York, they were generally met at the dock by Tammany members, who provided them with help to deal with a strange city. This often included a place to live, food and clothing if they needed it and a job. Tammany also enabled the immigrants to rapidly become new citizens. Out of gratitude, they generally voted for the candidates whom the Tammany Society supported.

But Tammany leaders weren't content to depend solely on these tactics to win elections. They also resorted to fraud. In poorer areas of the city, like Five Points on the Lower East Side, they employed gangs of thugs to intimidate voters who might support opposition candidates. These thugs would keep voters away from the polls. To add even more votes for their own candidates, Tammany officials would stand at the voting booths and stuff fake ballots into each voting box.

Once the Tammany candidates were in office, they often began lining their pockets with money taken for doing favors. This illegal practice is called graft. In 1851, Tweed was elected an alderman. The mayor and the aldermen ran the city. There were forty of these aldermen, who were nicknamed the "forty thieves." If a businessman wanted to open a new ferry line across New York Harbor, he would bribe the aldermen to give him a license to do it. If another entrepreneur hoped to build a new streetcar line along one of New York's long avenues, he would need to bribe the aldermen as well.

Aldermen made money in other ways, too. The cost in the contract for a new project, such as street repair, would be higher than the price necessary to do the job. After the contractor was paid, the aldermen would put the rest of the money in their pockets. Since almost every official was involved in the graft, nobody tried to stop it.

From his position as alderman, Tweed gradually increased his power in the city. By the post-Civil War period, he was known as "Boss" Tweed. As boss, Tweed picked the Democratic candidates for mayor and aldermen. He controlled all city contracts. He also raised graft and corruption to a level never before seen in New York.

"You know what I don't understand," Nast said to a reporter at *Harper's* one afternoon as they sat together smoking cigars. "People know how corrupt this city is. Why do they allow Tweed to get away with it?"

"Apathy, I suppose," the reporter answered. "People like to complain a lot but they never do anything."

"Tweed's also bought himself a lot of support," Nast said with a disgusted shrug. "Look at all those people lining their pockets from the contracts he gives them."

"Or the jobs they get on the city payroll," the reporter added. "Tweed is so powerful, there's no one out there who can stop him."

"Oh yes, there is," the cartoonist said, smiling. Thomas Nast."

In one of his early cartoons portraying Tweed's activities, Nast showed the varieties of corruption that the Tammany Society had let loose on the city. More and more immigrants were becoming citizens much faster than the law allowed so they could vote for Tweed and his candidates. Saloons were permitted to stay open on Sundays, in violation of the laws. But their owners had to support Tammany. Those who didn't were shut down. Police were preventing honest voters from casting their ballots against Tammany politicians. And widespread ballot-box stuffing was permitted at every election.

At first, no one seemed to pay much attention to Nast. Only the *New York Times* seemed to share his opinion of Tweed. Most other newspapers denounced *Harper's* and the *Times* as Republican papers that only wanted to bring down the Democratic boss. Meanwhile, New Yorkers smiled at Nast's caricatures of Tweed —

To be a citizen of New York is a disgrace.... The New Yorker belongs to a community worse governed by lower and baser blackguard scum than any city in Western Christendom.

—George Templeton Strong, diarist, 1868

Thomas Nast did quite a few drawings of Boss Tweed and his "henchmen." In this illustration, district attorney Peter Sweeney stands alongside Tweed, who displays a huge diamond pin on his chest. In back of Tweed is city comptroller Richard Connolly with New York Mayor A. Oakley Hall, just coming out of the elevator.

the big, bloated boss wearing a medallion with the ferocious tiger, which had become the symbol of Tammany Hall. Nast drew Tweed surrounded by his henchmen. There was the city district attorney, an Irishman with a big mustache named Peter Sweeney. Another Irishman, Richard "Slippery Dick" Connolly, was the city comptroller. A fat man, he always stood near Tweed. A fourth member of the ring was the mayor of

NOBODY'S PERFECT

Thomas Nast attacked Tweed and his cronies because they were corrupt. But he also opposed Tammany Hall, because so many of its members were Irish Catholics. Like many other Americans in the 19th century, Nast feared that the Catholics were loyal to a foreign power rather than the United States. That power was represented by the pope in Rome. But this was a prejudice that had no basis in fact. "He was absolutely merciless in his attacks upon those with whom he disagreed," explained his grandson Thomas Nast St. Hill. "Communists, corrupt politicians . . .and even the Catholic Church were among those upon whom he vented his wrath."

New York, A. Oakley Hall, who was always shown wearing huge glasses.

Almost daily an article appeared in the pages of the *Times* attacking Tweed and his corrupt ring of politicians. And Nast regularly contributed cartoons to *Harper's* lampooning the boss. Tweed is portrayed with a large diamond on his chest — a $15,000 stone that he had bought with graft money. He also built a magnificent $350,000 mansion on Fifth Avenue. In one cartoon, Tweed is shown sitting in front of his mansion while New

THREE BLIND MICE! SEE HOW THEY RUN!
THE *Times* CUT OFF THEIR TAILS WITH A CARVING-KNIFE.

One favorite cartoon published in Harper's Weekly, *"Three Blind Mice," focused on men who headed the committee investigating Boss Tweed.*

York's poor are unable to pay their apartment rents. Nast's caption reads: "The rich growing richer, the poor growing poorer."

When a committee of business leaders was appointed to investigate the city finances, they reported that there was no corruption. Apparently, these businessmen were so afraid that Tweed would no longer give them any new contracts, they didn't want to criticize him. Nast was very upset by the committee report. He drew a cartoon of the "three blind mice" to symbolize the three men who headed the committee.

Boss Tweed was so angry at Nast for his cartoons that he tried to put pressure on *Harper's* to stop them. The company that owned the magazine also published textbooks for the city schools. Tweed took away their contract to supply the books and gave it to another company, which he controlled. But *Harper's* told Nast to continue his assault on Tweed. Eventually it would bring him down.

Points to Ponder

◆ Why do you think the voters of New York let the Tweed Ring take over and control city government?

◆ What qualities did Nast need to stand up to Boss Tweed and his ring?

Chapter 5

THE FALL
OF BOSS TWEED

According to an old saying, "There's no honor among thieves." It was treachery by one of Tweed's own former lieutenants that eventually brought the downfall of the boss and his gang.

James O'Brien had been a New York City sheriff. He had left his position when Tweed refused to give him his share of graft money. O'Brien was very angry at the boss, but he bided his time and eventually took his revenge. O'Brien arranged to have a friend appointed to a job in the city comptroller's office. Once inside, the friend collected evidence on the Tweed Ring's dishonest financial dealings and gave it to O'Brien.

Until then, neither the *Times* nor Nast had any hard figures to prove what Tweed and his cronies were doing. That would all change one summer night in 1871, when O'Brien took his evidence to Louis Jennings, editor of the *Times.*

"Hot night," O'Brien said as he entered Jennings's office.

"Warm," Jennings answered.

"You and Tom Nast have had a tough fight," O'Brien commented.

"Still have," Jennings said.

"I said had." O'Brien handed him an envelope. "Here's proof to back up all that the *Times* has charged."

What Jennings saw must have astounded him. It is estimated that the Tweed Ring may have stolen as much as $300 million from the city.

In July, 1871, the *Times* began publishing stories about the gigantic swindles. Tweed immediately sent someone to the publisher to bribe him. "Slippery Dick" Connolly offered *Times* publisher George Jones $5 million to stop printing the stories. He refused.

But even more than the *Times*, Tweed feared Nast. The little cartoonist published a picture showing the boss and his cronies using the contractors as front men to steal millions from New York. In the same cartoon Tweed is standing in a circle with his lieutenants and the contractors — each accusing the other of pocketing the money.

Let's stop them d—d pictures. I don't care so much what the papers write about me — my constituents can't read; but . . . they can see pictures!

—William M. Tweed, 1871

Since many of the people who voted for Tweed were immigrants who didn't understand English, he realized that Nast's pictures were worth more than a thousand words. Tweed tried to bribe Nast. He sent a banker, who was friendly to the ring, with an offer from an anonymous group of businessmen. They were prepared to offer him $100,000 so he could study painting in Europe.

"You need study and you need rest," the banker said. "Besides, this ring business will get you in trouble."

Tom decided to have some fun with the banker. "Don't you think I could get $500,000 to make the trip?"

The banker immediately agreed. "You can get $500,000 in gold to drop this ring business and get out of the country."

But Nast would have none of it. "I made up my mind long ago to put some of those fellows behind bars, and I'm going to put them there," he said.

"Only be careful, Mr. Nast," the banker warned him, "that you do not first put yourself into a coffin."

There were more threats on Nast's life and his home was under surveillance by the ring. In August, *Harper's* published a portrait of Nast, calling him the "most cordially hated man in New York — hated by men whose friendship would be a dishonor."

In September, reform groups met at the large Cooper Union hall in New York and demanded that Tweed and his henchmen be voted out of office by the people of the city. Later that month, a committee including some of these same reformers was about to seize the records of Comptroller Connolly. The day before the scheduled seizure, a break-in had mysteriously occurred at Connolly's office and the records were stolen. Nast published a scathing cartoon showing Tweed, Connolly, Sweeney and Hall side-by-side and claiming to know nothing about the break-in.

In November 1871, New York was facing an election. If Tweed could somehow convince the voters that the

WHO STOLE THE PEOPLE'S MONEY?" — DO TELL . N.Y.TIMES.   'TWAS HIM.

This cartoon was published in the New York Times *on August 19, 1871, and was entitled "Who Stole the People's Money?"*

statements made by Nast and the *Times* were false, he might be able to hold onto his power. The boss still believed he would win. In a cartoon for *Harper's* just before the election, Nast portrayed a bloated Tweed with a huge moneybag instead of a head. The boss stood defiantly with his hands thrust in his pockets, daring the voters to turn him out of office.

In fact, many New Yorkers were planning to do just that. A committee of reformers examining the city's finances published its report before the election. It substantiated the facts that had been printed in the *Times.*

Meanwhile, there had been a falling-out among the leaders of the Tweed Ring. Sweeney, Tweed and Hall had decided to blame all the corruption on "Slippery Dick" Connolly. He refused to be the scapegoat and agreed to cooperate in a full investigation of the ring.

At election time, Nast published a scathing cartoon showing a huge Tammany tiger in the Roman Coliseum devouring Columbia, the symbol of liberty. In the viewing stands sat the emperor — William Marcy Tweed.

But the tiger and Tweed proved to be no match for the voters of New York. The Tammany Society politicians were turned out of office. And Tweed was arrested.

Tweed immediately put up bail so he could stay out of jail and begin his defense. Connolly was also out on bail. But before his trial began, Connolly escaped to Europe. Meanwhile, Sweeney left the country and fled to France before the courts could catch up with him. Tweed finally came to trial in January 1873. But the jury couldn't agree on a conviction.

"I am tired of the whole farce," Tweed said. "No jury will ever convict me." But he was wrong. At his second trial, in November, the jury did convict him and he was sentenced to twelve years in jail. Tweed was not treated like other prisoners, however. He was allowed to visit his home and have dinner with his wife. On one of these visits, Tweed escaped and hid out in New Jersey. Then he slipped aboard a ship headed for Cuba and eventually went to Spain.

Unfortunately for him, the Spanish authorities had a picture of Tweed drawn by Thomas Nast. They captured the former boss, and returned him to New York. Tweed eventually died in prison.

Meanwhile, Nast's reputation soared. He had become the most famous illustrator in America. And the circulation of *Harper's* had tripled, due in large part to his successful campaign against Tweed.

Mr. Nast has carried political illustrations to a pitch of excellence never before attained in this country, and has secured for them an influence on opinion such as they never came near having in any country.

—The Nation, 1871

Points to Ponder

◆ Do you think it was fair for Nast to portray Tweed and his friends the way he did?

◆ Put yourself in Nast's place during his campaign against the Tweed Ring. How would you feel being threatened by Tweed? Would you have been tempted by the bribe?

Chapter 6

✤

AN ARTIST'S WORLD

ith Tweed safely removed from office, Thomas Nast was being hailed for his courage and honesty across America. He was not yet thirty-five, but Nast had exhausted himself in the long campaign against Tweed, sometimes drawing as many as three pictures a week. In 1873, he and his wife, Sarah, sailed to Europe for a vacation. Aboard ship, he met a promoter named James Redpath who made him an intriguing offer. He suggested that Nast should cash in on his fame by going on an illustrated lecture tour. He would be billed as the "Prince of Caricaturists — The Destroyer of Tammany Hall." At first, Nast declined. The thought of standing up and speaking in front of a large group of people made him extremely nervous. But Redpath persisted. He promised that Nast could earn as much as $20,000 from a single lecture season. It meant financial security for his family — a prospect too important for Nast to turn down.

His first lecture was in Peabody, Massachusetts, on October 6, 1873. Nast was suffering from a severe case of stage fright and must have wondered how he had let Redpath talk him into this terrible situation.

"You got me into this scrape; you'll have to get on the platform with me," Nast told Redpath.

Of course, the promoter declined. He knew Nast could do it on his own. The lecture was a success. And Nast went on to Boston and later New York, where he spoke to huge crowds. He talked about how he had a hand in bringing down the Tweed gang and showed the crowd many of his famous drawings. After a seven-month tour he had exceeded Redpath's wildest predictions — earning $40,000 at a time when an average worker considered himself lucky to earn $1,000 a year.

However, Nast didn't delude himself into believing he was a great speaker or that he should quit *Harper's* and join the lecture circuit. Throughout his career, Nast always had the ability to sit back and laugh at his own shortcomings. He regularly drew amusing caricatures of himself—a short, fat, bearded artist wielding his pencil. Nast was an artist, and he knew that drawing pictures made him the happiest.

By the middle of the 1870s, Nast seemed to realize that the political landscape was changing. In 1877, Ulysses Grant left the White House. Even Nast had to admit that the scandals during Grant's administration had greatly damaged the Republican Party. That same year, Republican Rutherford B. Hayes became president after a very close election. There were cries of fraud against both sides during the voting. And eventually a special commission had to determine the winner of the election. In his commentary on the presidential race, Nast depicted the Republican Party as a huge elephant with a bandage around its head and its arm in a sling. Under the picture was the caption: "Another such victory and I am undone."

Nast chose the elephant as a symbol of the Republicans to illustrate that the party had become a large, bloated beast with no sense of direction. He believed that the Republican spirit of reform was passing. In the South, for example, he saw that the commitment to help African Americans had ended. Many of them had become sharecroppers, working for their former owners on cotton plantations at miserable wages. And, over the next

"ANOTHER SUCH VICTORY AND I AM UNDONE."—Pyrrhus

Commenting on the presidential race, Nast depicted the "wounded" Republican Party in a drawing for Harper's Weekly *on March 24, 1877, with the caption "Another Such Victory and I Am Undone."*

decades, a series of laws would be passed that produced a terrible system of racial segregation.

Of course, Nast had no confidence that the Democratic Party would do any better. To symbolize the Democrats, he created the donkey. This beast was even more stubborn and less intelligent than the elephant.

Unfortunately, many voters did not seem to share Nast's concern with the state of American politics. Their attention was elsewhere. This has been called the "Gilded Age" of the nation's history. Great fortunes were being made by industrialists like Andrew Carnegie and John D. Rockefeller. Such men built great marble mansions and entertained lavishly at gala parties that their envious fellow citizens wanted to read about. Although it was a period of bitter labor strife in factories and mills, the middle-class readers of America's magazines were confident and comfortable. The reunited nation had settled into a period of rapid economic growth and seemed destined for greatness.

As the times changed, readers of *Harper's* wanted something different from the magazine. They were no longer interested in seeing it wage heated political battles. Readers' tastes had shifted more to family problems, human interest stories and literary fiction. Nast's biting political satire seemed out of step. When he started lampooning President Hayes, Nast's editor George William Curtis told him to stop. The artist caricatured his own predicament. He showed Uncle Sam trying to prevent him from creating any more cartoons that criticized the president of the United States. (By the way, Uncle Sam was another of Nast's wonderful creations.)

Although he was a relatively well-to-do man by the late 1870s, his cartoons were already beginning to appear less often in the magazine. He and Curtis did not see eye to eye on many issues, especially if they had to do with politics. On a couple of occasions, Nast even took a leave from *Harper's* and traveled abroad. There were also offers for him to go back on the lecture circuit, but in each case he turned them down.

In 1884, following another leave of absence, Nast returned just in time for a presidential election. The Republican presidential candidate was James G. Blaine. He seemed so corrupt to Nast and the editors at Harper's that they broke with a long-standing tradition. For the first time, they endorsed a Democratic nominee for President — Grover Cleveland, the governor of New York. Although Nast was roundly condemned by the Republican Party, his own strong sense of what was right would not let him support Blaine. Cleveland was eventually elected.

It was the last time Nast would play a prominent role in a presidential election. In 1886, he resigned from *Harper's*. His popularity belonged to another era. He no longer possessed the power and fame that had been his just over a decade earlier. In one of his final cartoons, he commented on the sad condition of American politics as he saw them. He drew a giant image of Boss Tweed looming over the country. Tweed was portrayed as a vulture sitting in his nest with bags of money in front of him. The caption read: "Our system of feathering nests breeds Tweeds all over the land."

March 27, 1886

Our System Of Feathering Nests Breeds Tweeds All Over The Land.

Thomas Nast drew Tweed as a vulture, perched on his nest of money, the caption reading, "Our System Of Feathering Nests Breeds Tweeds All Over The Land." The published date was March 27, 1886.

Points to Ponder

◆ What did Nast mean by this last cartoon?

◆ How does money corrupt government?

◆ Do you think politics will ever be made totally free of corruption?

◆ What does Nast's experience tell us about fame and popularity?

Chapter 7

✤

A FORGOTTEN MAN

In the years after he left *Harper's,* Thomas Nast found himself adrift. He tried the lecture circuit again, but he was no longer famous enough to attract large audiences. Occasionally, Nast was contacted by a newspaper that was starting up and asked to contribute a cartoon. The editors believed that a picture by the once famous Thomas Nast might improve their readership. But Nast's association with these publications never lasted very long. He would never again achieve his former prominence.

In 1889, *Harper's* asked Nast to collect pictures of Santa Claus and Christmas that he had produced over the years. These were published as the book *Christmas Drawings for the Human Race.* One pair of pictures shows a young girl talking with Santa Claus over the telephone, which had been invented by Alexander Graham Bell in 1875.

Meanwhile, Nast began to devote more of his time to painting. Earlier in his career, while he was still a famous cartoonist, Nast had also painted pictures. Some of Nast's later paintings feature scenes from the Civil War. He created them in his studio on the second floor of his Morristown, New Jersey, house. A pet mockingbird shared the studio with Nast. During the day, the artist would whistle at the bird, who, in turn, would whistle back at him.

One of the best-known pictures Nast created was General Robert E. Lee's surrender to General Grant at Appomattox in 1865 — an event that ended the Civil War. This painting had been commissioned to mark the thirtieth anniversary of the surrender in 1895. Perhaps it was fitting that Nast returned to the period when his fame as an artist had begun, and to one of his heroes — Ulysses S. Grant.

Nast received several other commissions to produce paintings, which enabled him to earn a modest income. But it was never enough to achieve financial security for his family. Nast was eventually forced to sell off the horses that he kept in the stables at his home. He even lacked

The last known portrait of Thomas Nast was taken in 1902.

money to pay a doctor or a dentist when he needed one. Nast would paint their portraits to give to them in lieu of paying their fees.

In 1900, Thomas Nast turned sixty. He was a gray-haired man, with a large mustache, who always wore a flower in the lapel of his jacket. With his wide hat, gold watch and silver-headed cane, Nast tried to maintain a look of success although he had fallen on hard times. In 1901, when his friend Theodore Roosevelt became president, Nast asked Roosevelt if he might be able to find a job for him in the government. About the only opening was a position as consul in Ecuador, located on the west coast of South America. Although Nast had no experience as a diplomat, he took the post. It paid an annual salary of $4,000.

Nast departed for Guayaquil in 1902, without his wife, Sarah. He was worried about her safety in Ecuador, where epidemics of yellow fever regularly broke out, causing many deaths. Once he arrived at his post in Guayaquil, Nast wrote home frequently. The seacoast of Guayaquil was hot and primitive. Nast desperately longed for his wife and his studio in Morristown.

"You say my poor old mockingbird misses me," Nast wrote sadly. "I am very sorry. I do miss him, poor fellow, and his mocking sounds."

During the fall, there were new outbreaks of yellow fever almost every day, resulting in the death of most of its victims. Nast wrote his wife optimistically that he was "too old to catch the fever." But he was mistaken. On December 7, 1902, the fever claimed him. Nast was just sixty-two years old.

Points to Ponder

◆ What qualities did Nast possess that made him successful?

◆ How could you apply these qualities in your own life — today and in the future?

◆ How was Nast able to deal with the disappointments that marked his later years?

Epilogue

SUMMING UP
A LIFE

W hen Thomas Nast died, his life had come full circle. He had been born poor in another land, and his parents had brought him to America to find a better life. Nast achieved it. He became famous because of his artistic talent and a willingness to always speak his mind — honestly, candidly and openly. He was not afraid to stand up for his beliefs and let America know where he stood. In doing this, he hoped to improve the American system of government. But fame and popularity are fleeting, as Nast learned. Eventually, he lost his position of influence and experienced financial hardships. Finally, he died in poverty, far from the shores of his beloved adopted country.

Nast's career was a classic American success story — one that exemplifies the qualities of honesty and courage. Part of the vast wave of European immigration that enriched our nation, Nast went to work at age fifteen on one of America's young newspapers, bringing to life the great events of the day for millions of readers. Within just a few years, the young artist played a pivotal role in persuading the people of the North to give total support to the effort to hold the Union together by force of arms. As Abraham Lincoln put it: "Thomas Nast has been our best recruiting sergeant."

After the Civil War, when America's great cities were mired in political corruption, Nast's scathing but humorous caricatures pricked the conscience of New Yorkers until they drove the most corrupt political machine of the era from office. Even in the face of bribes and threats Nast never let up until the Tweed Ring was destroyed. "I try to hit the enemy between the eyes and knock him down," Nast said.

Although at his death he was all but forgotten by his countrymen, Nast's forthright portrayal of graft and corruption made his a life worth living, and ensured that he would be honored a century after his death for the example he set for fearless and honest journalists everywhere.

Afterword

❖

TO PARENTS

hat does Thomas Nast's life teach us? Uncompromising honesty is essential in the pursuit of truth. Nast's honesty often seemed to carry a high price. His life was threatened. Most of his newspaper colleagues laughed at him and criticized him for pursuing Boss Tweed. Some thought he was a naïve Don Quixote, others considered him a fool. But in the end, Nast's persistence exposed the truth.

You may wish to discuss with your child the courage it takes to stand up for one's convictions. We often applaud an honest person who is successful. But we forget how lonely and difficult it can be to voice our beliefs when everybody else disagrees with us or thinks our cause is hopeless. Give examples from your own experience and encourage your son or daughter to offer his or her own stories.

You might also talk about parallels between Nast's newspaper career and that of journalists today. Do they keep to the same standards of honesty in exposing political corruption? Has our political system improved since the time of Nast? How successful would Nast be if he were alive today? Encourage your child to think about the truth of what he reads and sees in the media, and teach him how to evaluate the biases or self-interest of the media, whether it's editorial or advertising material.

Finally, you may want to draw parallels between the pursuit of truth in the political arena and the way people seek it in different fields. Scientists or inventors, for example, often spend years finding the cure for a disease or trying to perfect a mechanical device. And they keep going, although many others may question the value of their work. How important are the qualities of honesty, courage and persistence for these individuals?

BIBLIOGRAPHY

Allen, Oliver. *The Tiger: The Rise and Fall of Tammany Hall.* Reading, MA: Addison-Wesley, 1993.

Callow, Alexander. *The Tweed Ring.* Westport, CT: Greenwood Press, 1966.

Keller, Morton. *The Art and Politics of Thomas Nast.* New York: Oxford, 1968.

Paine, Albert Bigelow. *Thomas Nast: His Period and His Pictures.* New York: Chelsea House, 1980.

St. Hill, Thomas. "The Life and Death of Thomas Nast." *American Heritage,* June 1971.

GLOSSARY

alderman. An elected member of a city's governing body.

caricature. A picture that exaggerates the people or events it portrays to create humor.

corruption. Dishonest activities, often by politicians, who accept illegal payments from people who want something from government, such as a contract to do work.

Don Quixote. A fictional Spanish knight who fought for honor and justice, but often against hopeless odds or against imaginary enemies. The name is often used to describe people fighting idealistic but silly or hopeless battles.

famine. An extreme scarcity of food that causes the deaths of many people.

graft. Money taken by a politician for illegally using power to provide favors.

henchman. A political supporter, accomplice or aide, often a dishonest one.

Ku Klux Klan. A racist organization founded by white Southerners in the 1860s with the goal of terrorizing African Americans and keeping them from gaining any political or economic power.

lampoon. To make fun of through satire.

lecture circuit. A tour around the country or around the world by a speaker who addresses paying audiences. Lectures were a popular form of entertainment in the days before movies and television.

political boss. A powerful political leader.

Reconstruction. The process of bringing Southern states back into the Union after the Civil War.

Tammany Hall. The headquarters of the Tammany Society, center of Democratic politics in New York during the nineteenth century.